eMoviePoster.com

presents

JOHN WAYNE MOVIE POSTERS AT AUCTION

Volume 22 of the illustrated history of movies through posters

Every item pictured in this book will be auctioned by
eMoviePoster.com on the Internet from 6/30/04-7/10/04 (all items will
close on 7/10 between 6 PM CST & 9 PM CST). Complete detailed
descriptions of every item (including high quality digital images and
detailed condition descriptions) can be found on
our website **http://www.emovieposter.com**

IN THIS AUCTION THERE ARE:

NO Buyer's Premiums
NO U.S. Shipping Charges
NO Sales Tax (except in Missouri)
See our website for full details!

IMPORTANT NOTICE:

In addition to the auction of the items in this volume,
THERE WILL BE ANOTHER REMARKABLE AUCTION OF MOVIE
POSTERS 7/1/04-7/11/04! Along with the items in this catalog,
eMoviePoster.com will auction an amazing collection of 592 movie
posters, lobby cards and glass slides from many of the finest movies
ever made, covering all years and genres! The auction runs from July
1st to July 11th (see our website for full details).

Edited and Published by Bruce Hershenson
P.O. Box 874, West Plains, MO 65775
Phone: **(417) 256-9616** Fax: **(417) 257-6948**
mail@brucehershenson.com (e-mail)
http://**www.emovieposter.com** (website)

THE WESTERN MOVIES OF JOHN WAYNE

Note that the movies are listed in the exact order they were released, with the exact opening date (if known) followed by the numbers of the items in this book from that film.

INDEX

INTRODUCTION

My name is Bruce Hershenson and since 1990 I have sold over 21 MILLION dollars of vintage movie posters, much of it through public auctions. In 1990 I organized the very first all-movie poster auction ever held by a major auction house and since then I organized 12 more major "live" movie poster auctions (nine more for Christie's auction house and three for Howard Lowery auctions) with total sales of just under ten million dollars. In between, I sold over 30,000 movie posters and lobby cards through semi-annual sales catalogs with sales of over four million dollars.

In 2001 I decided to move my major auctions to the Internet. On June 30 and July 1, 2001 (in Vintage Hollywood Posters IV), I auctioned 711 items for a total of $717,000. Those who have purchased items at other major auctions are all too familiar with the many added fees tacked on after the auction,s close, including a buyer's premium that ranges from 15% to 20%, and shipping fees that range from high to outrageous. But in THIS auction, Vintage Hollywood Posters IV, there were NO Buyer's Premium, NO U.S. Shipping charges, and NO Sales Tax (except in Missouri). This saved most buyers from 30% to 40%!

I also provided complete detailed descriptions of every item. Many major auctions only provide bidders with fuzzy images and fuzzier condition descriptions, glossing over condition defects and restoration. I provided high quality digital images, and detailed condition descriptions (including detailed descriptions of each restored item's PRE-restoration condition, something NO other major auction house provides). In 2002 and 2003 I repeated the process with Vintage Hollywood Posters V & VI, with combined sales of just over one million dollars!

Most of my major auctions have been wide-ranging assortments of movie posters, covering all years and genres. Twice I have been consigned comprehensive collections focused on a single subject (once serial movie posters and once 1950s sci-fi movie posters). NOW I PRESENT MY THIRD MAJOR AUCTION DEVOTED TO A SINGLE SUBJECT.

This auction is comprised of an amazing collection of 334 movie posters, lobby cards and glass slides from EVERY western movie John Wayne ever made, including an example of almost every one-sheet movie poster known to exist (original and re-release)! The collection was assembled over decades, but every item in it will be auctioned on July 10, 2004.

This auction, JOHN WAYNE MOVIE POSTERS AT AUCTION, will end on 7/10/04 (there will be preliminary bidding from June 30-July 10). As will all my previous major online auctions, THERE ARE NO BUYER'S PREMIUMS, NO U.S. SHIPPING CHARGES AND NO SALES TAX (except in Missouri), which will again save buyers 30% to 40%!

IMPORTANT NOTICE: In addition to the action of the items in this volume, THERE WILL ALSO BE A REMARKABLE AUCTION OF MOVIE POSTERS, GLASS SLIDES AND LOBBY CARDS FROM 7/1/04-7/11/04! Along with the items in this catalog, eMoviePoster.com will auction an amazing collection of 592 movie posters, lobby cards and glass slides from many of the finest movies ever made, covering all years and genres! The auction runs from July 1st to July 11th (see our website for full details).

AN IMPORTANT ANNOUNCEMENT REGARDING THE POSTERS AND LOBBY CARDS IN THIS VOLUME!

All of the items pictured in this book will be auctioned by eMoviePoster.com on the Internet on 7/10/04. If you are reading this PRIOR to that date, go to http://www.emovieposter.com to find out how to bid (if you don't have Internet access, call 417 256 9616 and we'll make arrangements for you to bid another way). If you are reading this AFTER 7/10/04, you will find a sheet added to this volume that gives the prices every item sold for. If you have items you would like us to consider for our future auctions, go to http://www.emovieposter.com/consign.htm and read our terms, or, if you don't have Internet access, call us or mail us a list of your posters (see the first page of this book for full contact info). If you are interested in buying movie posters or lobby cards, or in learning more about the hobby, you should visit our website at http://www.emovieposter.com, where you will find thousands of images of the very best movie posters, as well as lots of information important to every collector.

PLEASE NOTE THAT ALL OF THE POSTERS IN THIS VOLUME ARE THE ORIGINAL RELEASE ONE-SHEET (27" X 41") MOVIE POSTER, UNLESS OTHERWISE NOTED. Also please note that the year on original posters may differ slightly from the year of first release (usually because the movie was released at the end of the year). Finally, please note that John Wayne posters are extremely rare, and it can be difficult to date some of them as to first issue or reissue, and as to exact date of release. We consulted the leading experts in the hobby as to the years of the posters, and also as to distinguishing originals from reissues. The listed information represents the consensus opinion of the leading experts in the hobby.

You can find out all you need to know about bidding on items in this most exciting auction by going to my website, http://www.emovieposter.com where you can also view this entire catalog in an online digital format.

Phillip Wages (who created my online auctions and also much of my website) and Amy Knight (who did the layouts and cover design for this book and many of my previous books) gave considerable assistance in the preparation of this auction and this book, and I thank them very much.

Bruce Hershenson
June 2004

1. THE BIG TRAIL, 1930 glass slide

2. THE BIG TRAIL, 1930 trade ad

4-11. ARIZONA, 1931 lobby cards

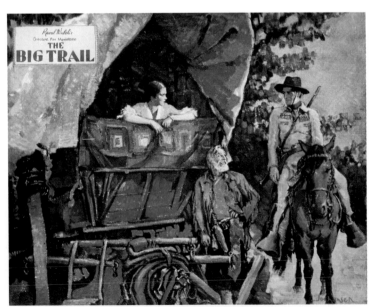

3. THE BIG TRAIL, 1930 lobby card

12. THE RANGE FEUD, 1931

13. THE SHADOW OF THE EAGLE, 1932, Chapter 5

16. TEXAS CYCLONE, 1932

14. THE SHADOW OF THE EAGLE, 1932 glass slide

15. THE SHADOW OF THE EAGLE,
1932, 1940s reissue

17. TWO FISTED LAW, 1932

18. THE HURRICANE EXPRESS, 1932, Chapter 1

19. THE HURRICANE EXPRESS, 1932,
Chapter 2

20. THE HURRICANE EXPRESS, 1932,
Chapter 4

21. THE HURRICANE EXPRESS, 1932,
Chapter 8

22. THE HURRICANE EXPRESS, 1932, Chapter 9

23. THE HURRICANE EXPRESS, 1932, Chapter 12

24. THE HURRICANE EXPRESS, 1932, 1940s reissue

25. RIDE HIM, COWBOY, 1932

26. RIDE HIM, COWBOY, 1932, 1939 reissue

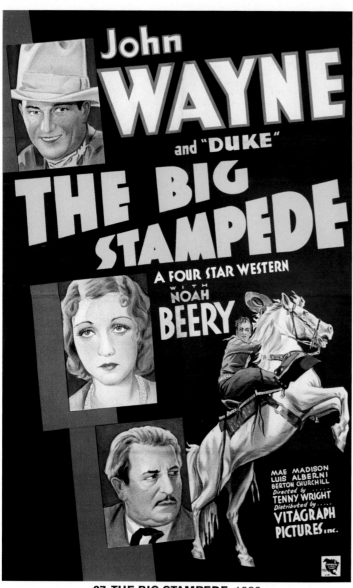

27. THE BIG STAMPEDE, 1932

28. HAUNTED GOLD, 1932

29. HAUNTED GOLD, 1932, c.1952 reissue

30-36. THE TELEGRAPH TRAIL, 1933
lobby cards

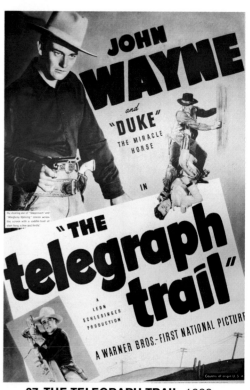

37. THE TELEGRAPH TRAIL, 1933,
1939 reissue

38. THE THREE MUSKETEERS, 1933, Chapter 1

39. THE THREE MUSKETEERS, 1933, Chapter 2

40. THE THREE MUSKETEERS, 1933, Chapter 1 glass slide

41. THE THREE MUSKETEERS, 1933, Chapter 3

42. THE THREE MUSKETEERS, 1933, Chapter 4

43. THE THREE MUSKETEERS, 1933, Chapter 5

44. THE THREE MUSKETEERS, 1933, Chapter 6

45. THE THREE MUSKETEERS, 1933, Chapter 8

46. THE THREE MUSKETEERS, 1933, Chapter 9

47. THE THREE MUSKETEERS, 1933, Chapter 10

48. THE THREE MUSKETEERS, 1933, Chapter 11

49. THE THREE MUSKETEERS, 1933, Chapter 12

50. SOMEWHERE IN SONORA, 1933

51. SOMEWHERE IN SONORA, 1933,
1939 reissue

52. THE MAN FROM MONTEREY, 1933 lobby card

53. THE MAN FROM MONTEREY, 1933

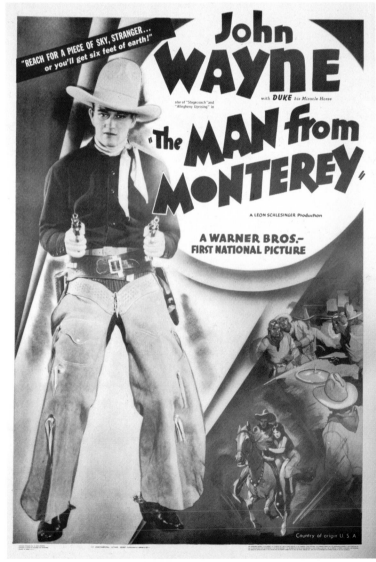

54. THE MAN FROM MONTEREY, 1933, 1939 reissue

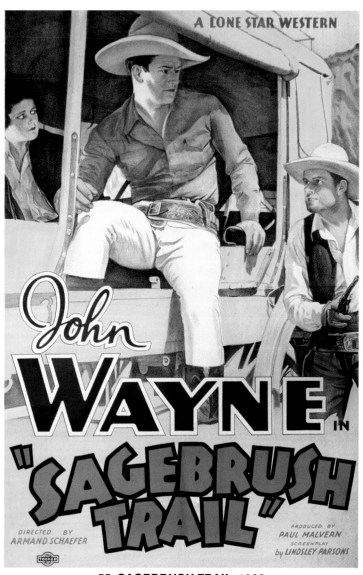

55. SAGEBRUSH TRAIL, 1933

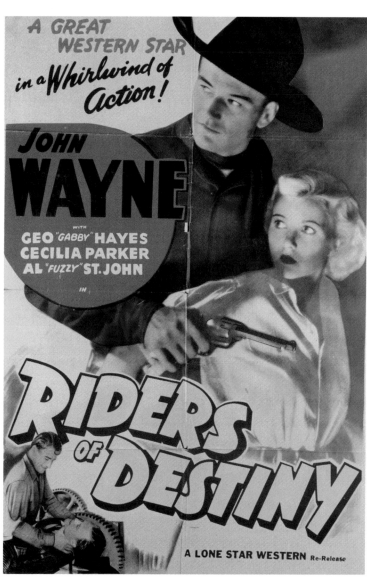

57. RIDERS OF DESTINY, 1933, c.1947 reissue

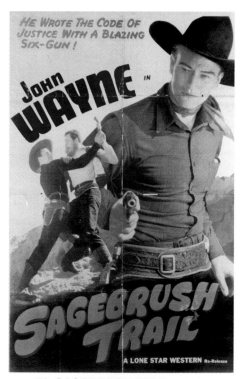

56. SAGEBRUSH TRAIL, 1933,
1940s reissue

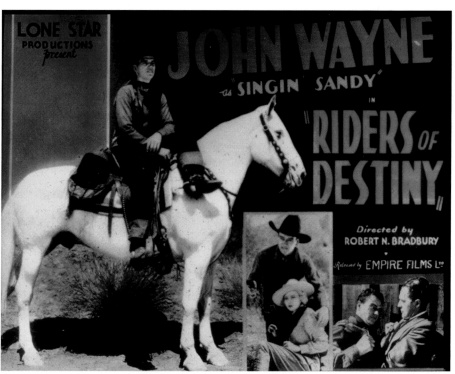

58. RIDERS OF DESTINY, 1933 glass slide

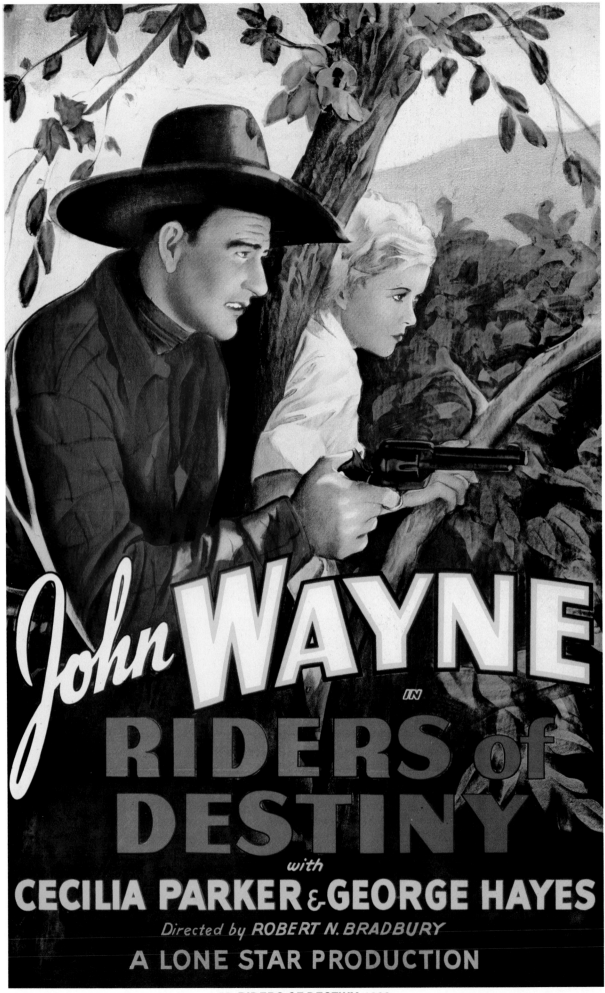

59. RIDERS OF DESTINY, 1933

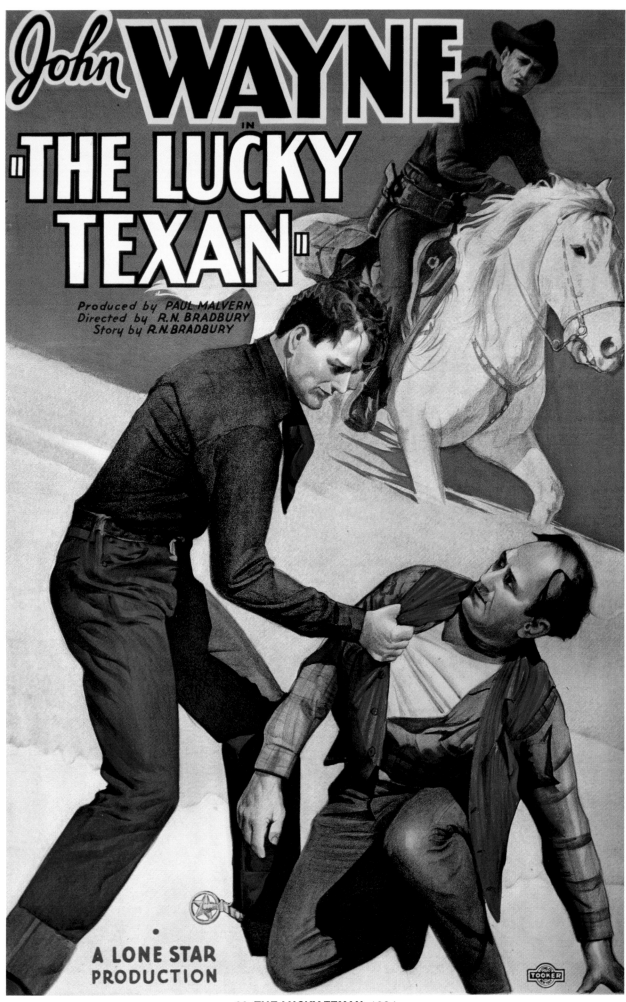

60. THE LUCKY TEXAN, 1934

61. THE LUCKY TEXAN, 1934 glass slide

62. WEST OF THE DIVIDE, 1934 glass slide

63. WEST OF THE DIVIDE, 1934

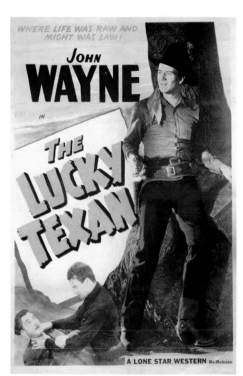

64. THE LUCKY TEXAN, 1934,
1940s reissue

65. WEST OF THE DIVIDE, 1934,
1939 reissue

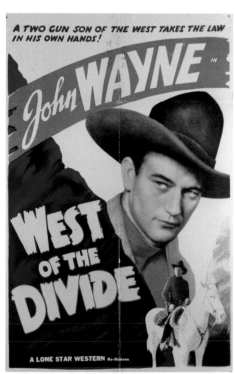

66. WEST OF THE DIVIDE, 1934,
1940s reissue

67. BLUE STEEL, 1934 glass slide

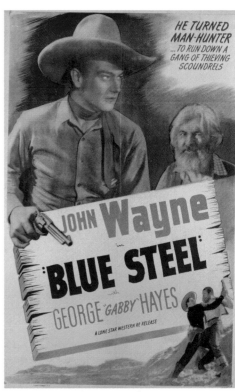

68. BLUE STEEL, 1934, 1940s reissue

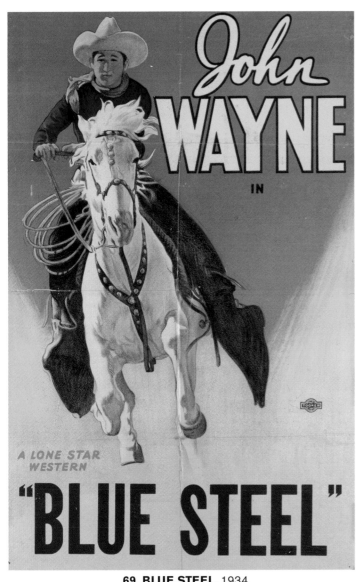

69. BLUE STEEL, 1934

70. THE MAN FROM UTAH, 1934, 1940s reissue

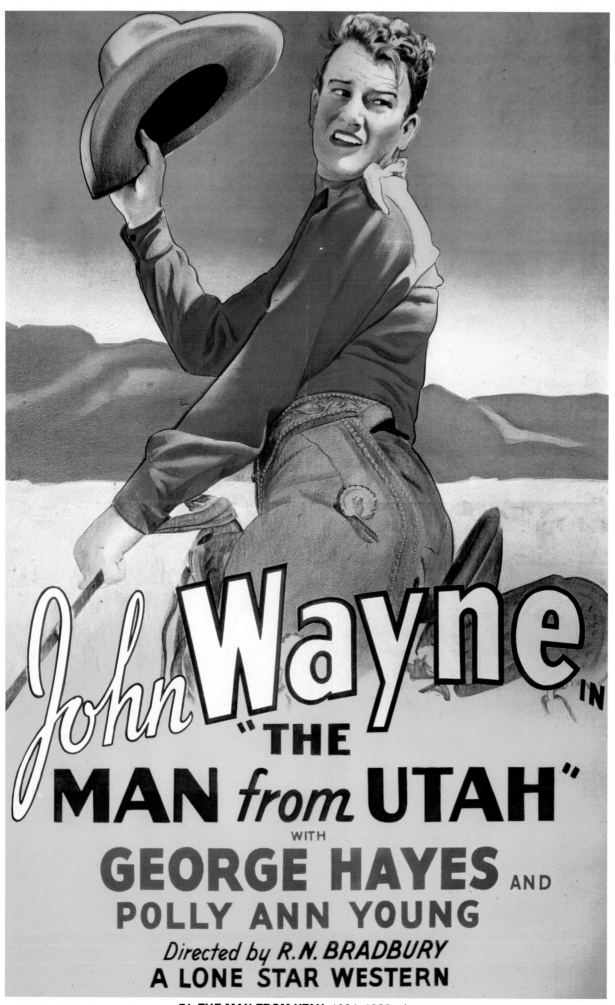

71. THE MAN FROM UTAH, 1934, 1939 reissue

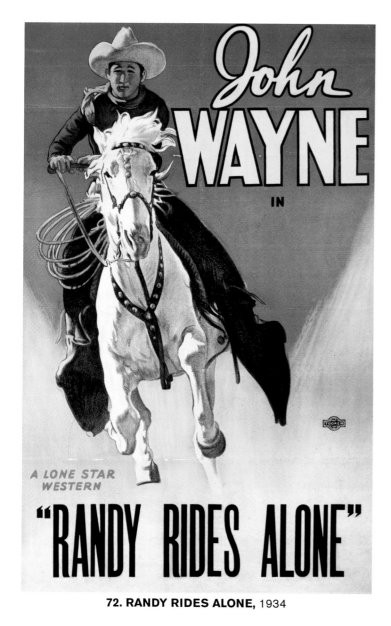

72. RANDY RIDES ALONE, 1934

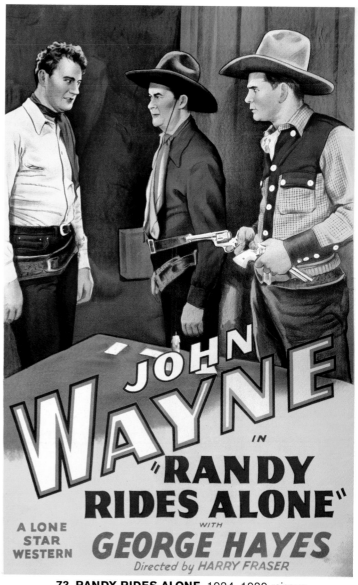

73. RANDY RIDES ALONE, 1934, 1939 reissue

74. THE STAR PACKER, 1934 glass slide

75. THE STAR PACKER, 1934, 1939 reissue

76. THE STAR PACKER, 1934

77. THE TRAIL BEYOND, 1934

78. THE TRAIL BEYOND, 1934 lobby card

79. THE TRAIL BEYOND, 1934 lobby card

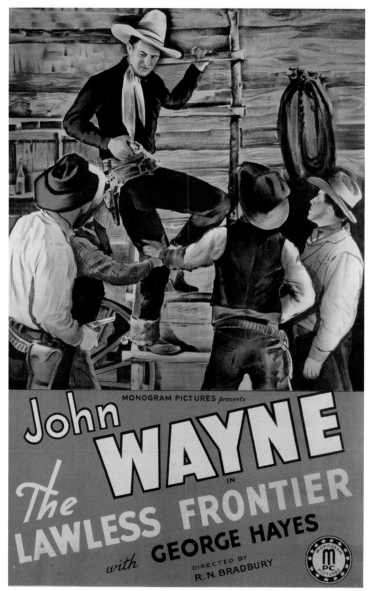

81. THE LAWLESS FRONTIER, 1934, 1939 reissue

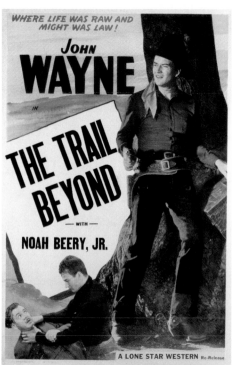

80. THE TRAIL BEYOND, 1934,
1940s reissue

82. THE LAWLESS FRONTIER, 1934, c.1939 reissue title card

83. THE LAWLESS FRONTIER, 1934

84. 'NEATH THE ARIZONA SKIES, 1934, 1939 reissue

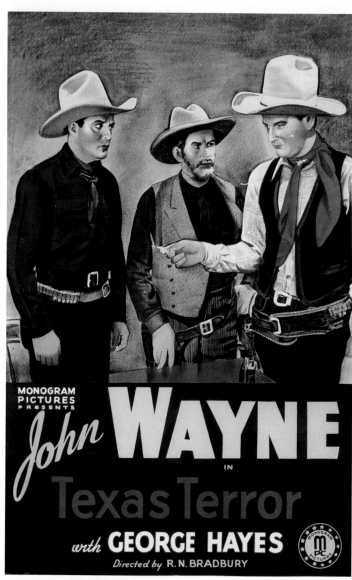

86. TEXAS TERROR, 1935, 1939 reissue

85. 'NEATH THE ARIZONA SKIES,
1934, 1940s reissue

87. TEXAS TERROR, 1935,
1940s reissue

88. RAINBOW VALLEY, 1935

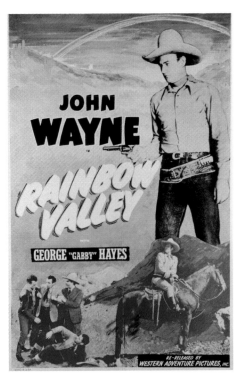

89. RAINBOW VALLEY, 1935,
1940s reissue

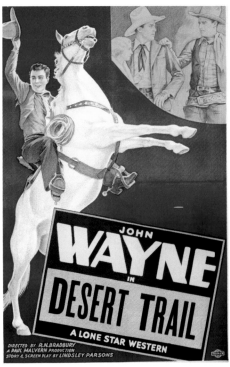

91. THE DESERT TRAIL, 1935

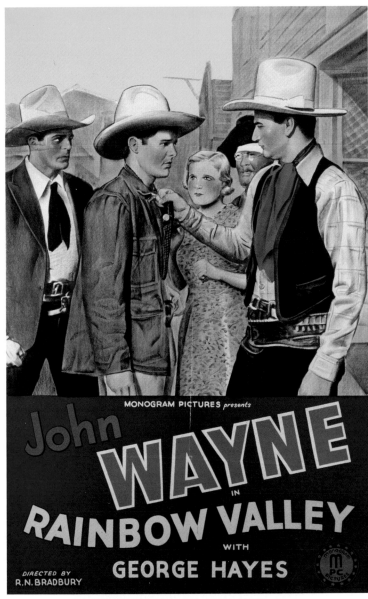

90. RAINBOW VALLEY, 1935, 1939 reissue

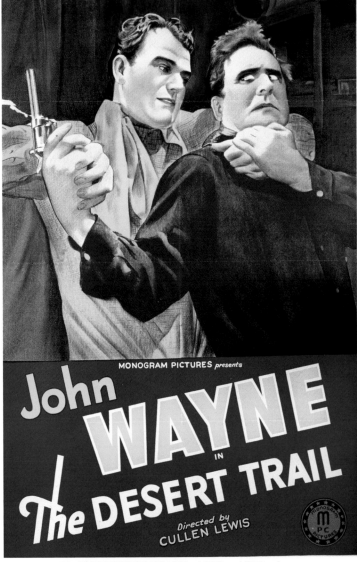

92. THE DESERT TRAIL, 1935, c.1939 reissue

93. THE DESERT TRAIL, 1935

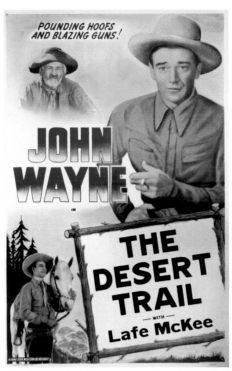

94. THE DESERT TRAIL, 1935,
1940s reissue

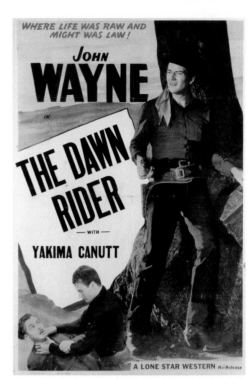

102. THE DAWN RIDER, 1935,
1940s reissue

95

96

97

98

99

100

101

95-101. THE DESERT TRAIL, 1935, c.1939 reissue lobby cards

103. THE DAWN RIDER, 1935

104. PARADISE CANYON, 1935 lobby card

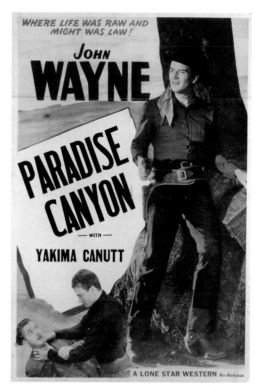

105. PARADISE CANYON, 1935,
1940s reissue

106. WESTWARD HO, 1935

107-111. WESTWARD HO, 1935 lobby cards

112. THE NEW FRONTIER, 1935

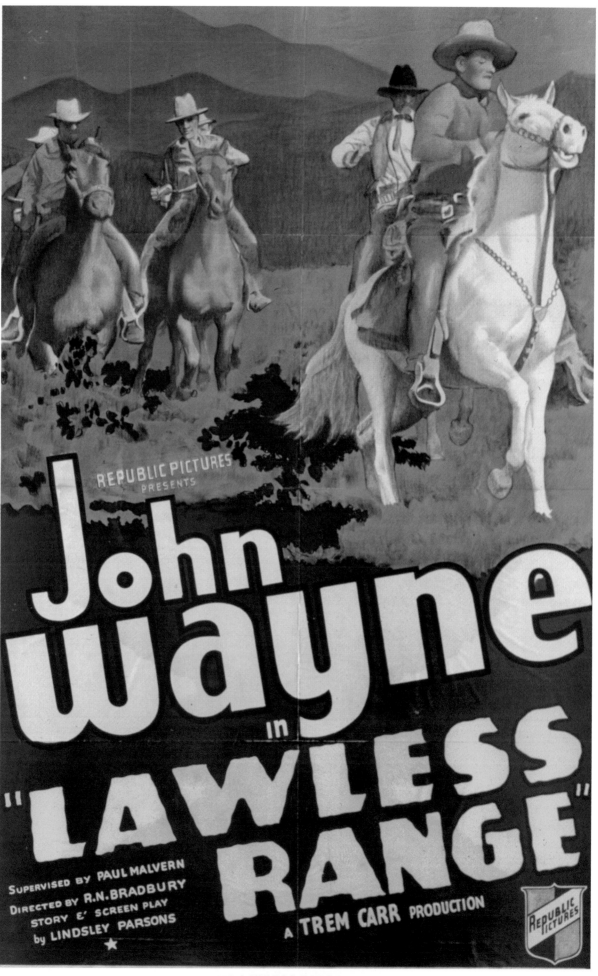

113. LAWLESS RANGE, 1935

114. THE OREGON TRAIL, 1936

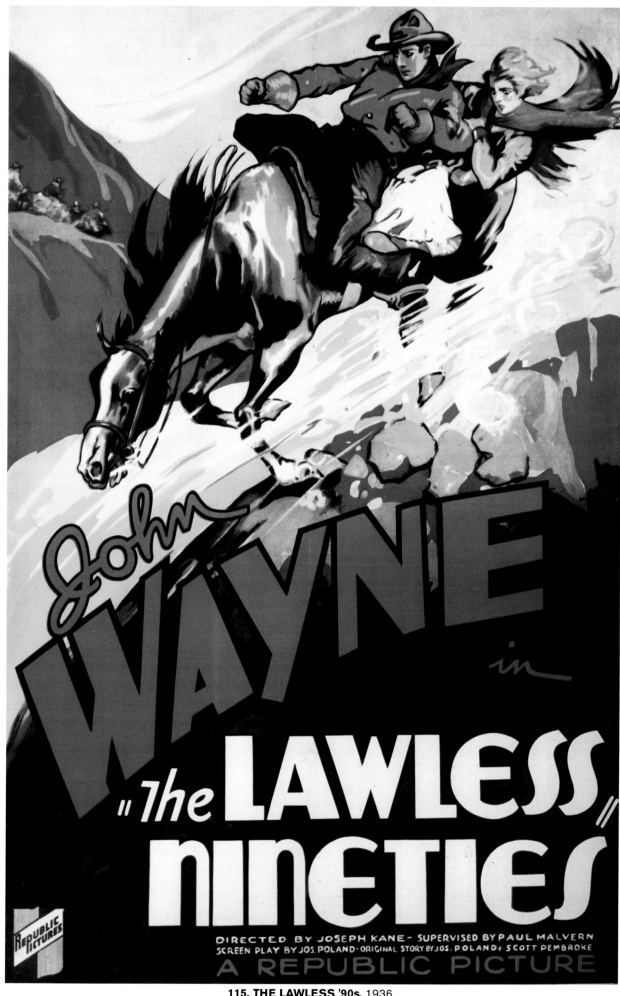

115. THE LAWLESS '90s, 1936

116. KING OF THE PECOS, 1936

117. THE LONELY TRAIL, 1936

118

119

120

121

122

123

118-123. THE LONELY TRAIL, 1936 lobby cards

124. WINDS OF THE WASTELAND, 1936

126. THE SEA SPOILERS, 1936

125. WINDS OF THE WASTELAND, 1936 lobby card

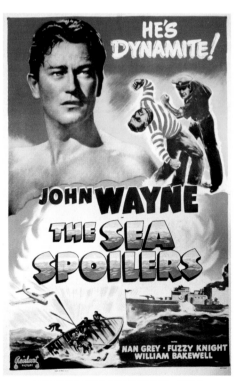

127. THE SEA SPOILERS, 1936,
1940s reissue

128. CONFLICT, 1936

130. CALIFORNIA STRAIGHT AHEAD, 1937

129. CONFLICT, 1936, 1949 reissue

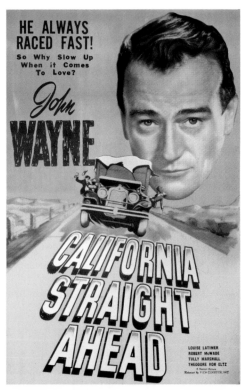

131. CALIFORNIA STRAIGHT AHEAD,
1937, 1948 reissue

132. I COVER THE WAR, 1937

135. ADVENTURE'S END, 1937

133. I COVER THE WAR, 1937, 1940s reissue

134. I COVER THE WAR, 1937 glass slide

136. ADVENTURE'S END, 1937, 1949 reissue

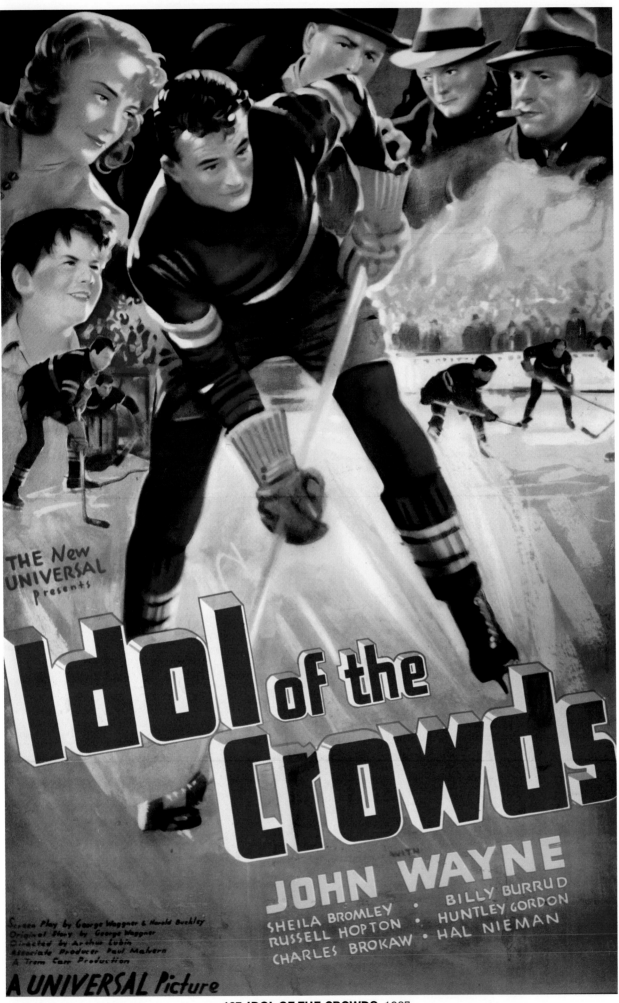

137. IDOL OF THE CROWDS, 1937

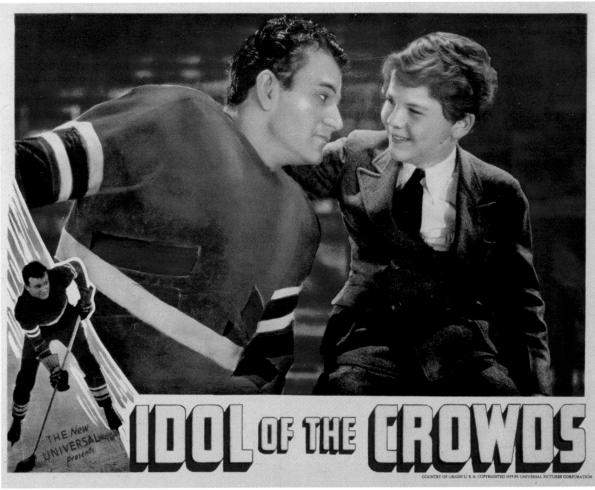

138-139. IDOL OF THE CROWDS, 1937 lobby cards

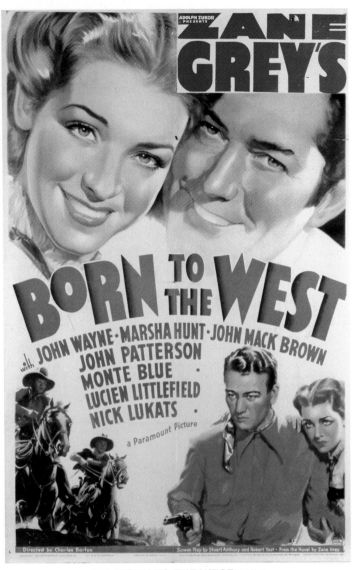

140. BORN TO THE WEST, 1937

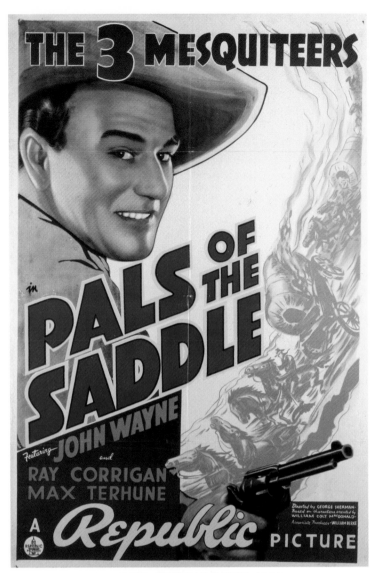

142. PALS OF THE SADDLE, 1938

141. BORN TO THE WEST, 1937,
1950 reissue

143. PALS OF THE SADDLE, 1938,
1953 reissue

144. OVERLAND STAGE RAIDERS, 1938

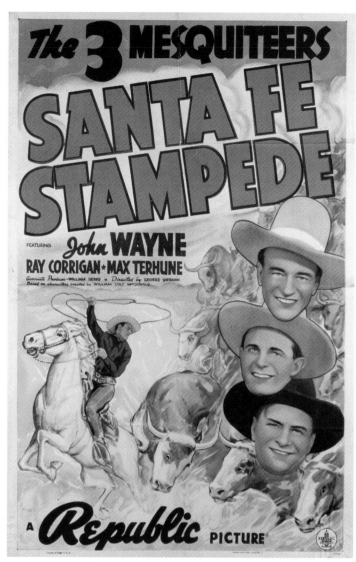

146. SANTA FE STAMPEDE, 1938

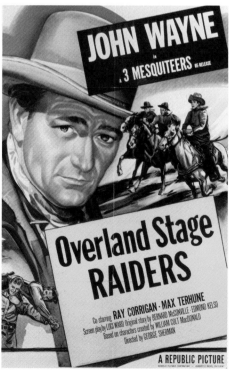

145. OVERLAND STAGE RAIDERS,
1938, 1953 reissue

147. SANTE FE STAMPEDE, 1938,
1953 reissue

148. RED RIVER RANGE, 1938

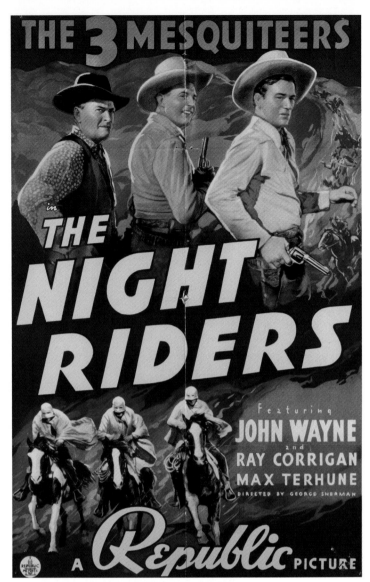

150. THE NIGHT RIDERS, 1939

149. RED RIVER RANGE, 1938,
1953 reissue

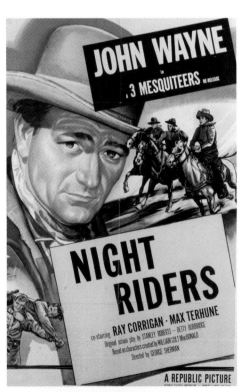

151. THE NIGHT RIDERS, 1939,
1953 reissue

STAGECOACH

A WALTER WANGER production • directed by JOHN FORD
with CLAIRE TREVOR • JOHN WAYNE • Andy Devine • John Carradine
Thomas Mitchell • Louise Platt • George Bancroft • Donald Meek
Berton Churchill • Tim Holt   Released thru United Artists

STAGECOACH

A WALTER WANGER production • directed by JOHN FORD
with CLAIRE TREVOR • JOHN WAYNE • Andy Devine • John Carradine
Thomas Mitchell • Louise Platt • George Bancroft • Donald Meek
Berton Churchill • Tim Holt   Released thru United Artists

152-153. STAGECOACH, 1939 lobby cards

154. STAGECOACH, 1939 Belgian poster

155. STAGECOACH, 1939, 1944 reissue

156. STAGECOACH, 1939, 1948 reissue

157. THREE TEXAS STEERS, 1939

158. THREE TEXAS STEERS, 1939, 1953 reissue

159. NEW FRONTIER, 1939

162. WYOMING OUTLAW, 1939

160. NEW FRONTIER, 1939 glass slide

161. NEW FRONTIER, 1939, 1953 reissue

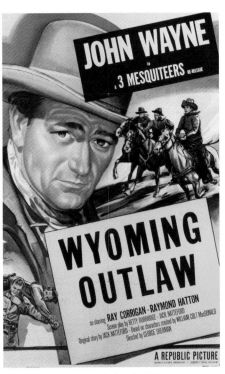

163. WYOMING OUTLAW, 1939, 1953 reissue

164. ALLEGHENY UPRISING, 1939

165. ALLEGHENY UPRISING, 1939 glass slide

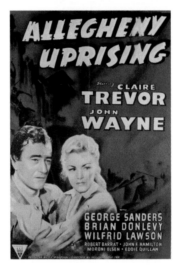

166. ALLEGHENY UPRISING,
1939, c.1952 reissue

167. ALLEGHENY UPRISING,
1939, c.1957 reissue

168. THE DARK COMMAND, 1940

169. THE DARK COMMAND, 1940

170. THE DARK COMMAND, 1940,
c.1952 reissue

171. THREE FACES WEST, 1940

174. THE LONG VOYAGE HOME, 1940

172. THREE FACES WEST, 1940,
1948 reissue

173. THREE FACES WEST,
1940 glass slide

175. THE LONG VOYAGE HOME,
1940 glass slide

176. THE LONG VOYAGE HOME, 1940,
c1948 reissue

177. SEVEN SINNERS, 1940

178. SEVEN SINNERS, 1940

179. SEVEN SINNERS, 1940, 1948 reissue

180. SEVEN SINNERS, 1940, 1953 reissue

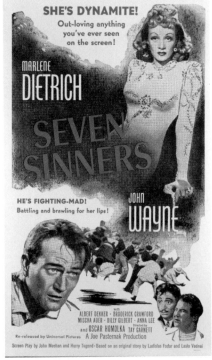

181. SEVEN SINNERS, 1940, 1950s reissue

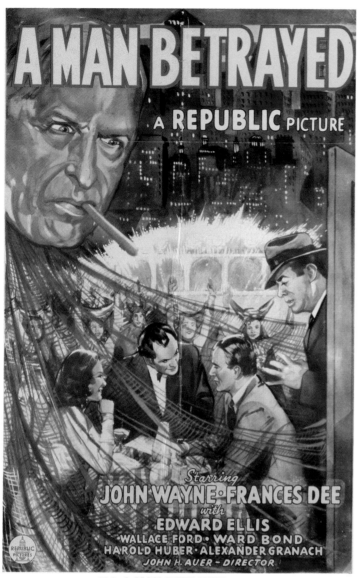

182. A MAN BETRAYED, 1941

185. LADY FROM LOUISIANA, 1941

186. LADY FROM LOUISIANA, 1941
glass slide

183. A MAN BETRAYED, 1941, 1953 reissue

184. A MAN BETRAYED, 1941 glass slide

187. LADY FROM LOUISIANA, 1941,
1953 reissue

188. THE SHEPHERD OF THE HILLS, 1941

190. LADY FOR A NIGHT, 1941

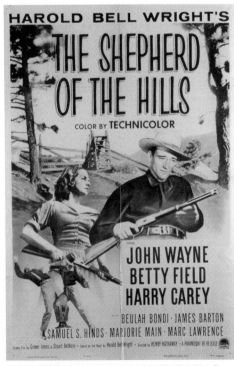

189. THE SHEPHERD OF THE HILLS,
1941, 1955 reissue

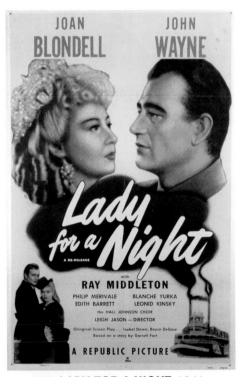

191. LADY FOR A NIGHT, 1941,
1950 reissue

192. REAP THE WILD WIND, 1942

193. REAP THE WILD WIND, 1942

194. REAP THE WILD WIND, 1942, 1954 reissue

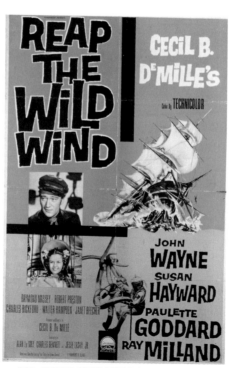

195. REAP THE WILD WIND, 1942, 1959 reissue

196. REAP THE WILD WIND, 1942, c.1964 reissue

197. THE SPOILERS, 1942

199. IN OLD CALIFORNIA, 1942

198. THE SPOILERS, 1942, 1940s reissue

200. IN OLD CALIFORNIA, 1942, 1940s reissue

201. IN OLD CALIFORNIA, 1942, 1940s reissue

202. FLYING TIGERS, 1942

203. FLYING TIGERS, 1942

204. FLYING TIGERS, 1942, 1948 reissue

205. FLYING TIGERS, 1942, 1954 reissue

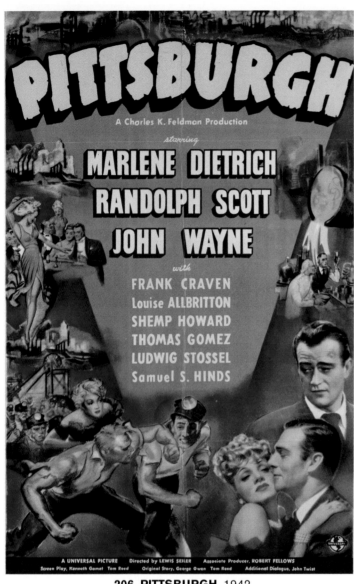

206. PITTSBURGH, 1942

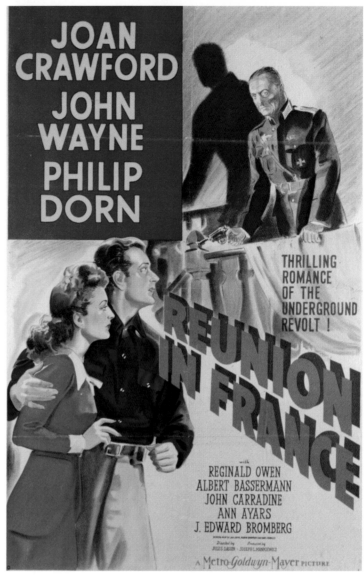

209. REUNION IN FRANCE, 1942

207. PITTSBURGH, 1942, 1948 reissue

208. PITTSBURGH, 1942, 1953 reissue

210. REUNION IN FRANCE, 1942

211. A LADY TAKES A CHANCE, 1943

212. A LADY TAKES A CHANCE, 1943,
1950 reissue

213. A LADY TAKES A CHANCE, 1943,
c.1954 reissue

214. IN OLD OKLAHOMA,
1943

217. THE FIGHTING SEABEES,
1944, 1954 reissue

215. IN OLD OKLAHOMA,
1943, 1940s reissue

216. IN OLD OKLAHOMA,
1943, 1959 reissue

218. THE FIGHTING SEABEES, 1944

219. TALL IN THE SADDLE, 1944

220. TALL IN THE SADDLE, 1944, 1949 reissue

221. TALL IN THE SADDLE, 1944, 1953 reissue

222. TALL IN THE SADDLE, 1944, 1957 reissue

223. FLAME OF BARBARY COAST, 1945

224. FLAME OF BARBARY COAST, 1945, 1950 reissue

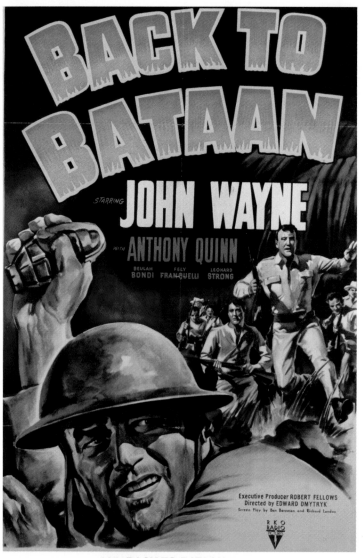

225. BACK TO BATAAN, 1945

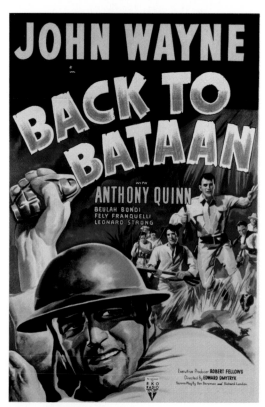

226. BACK TO BATAAN, 1945, 1950 reissue

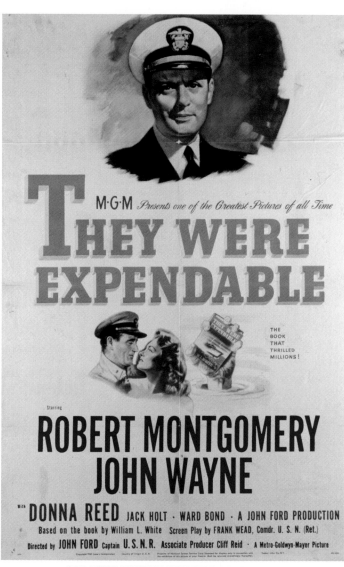

227. THEY WERE EXPENDABLE, 1945

228. THE THEY WERE EXPENDABLE, 1945, c.1950s reissue

229. DAKOTA, 1945

230. WITHOUT RESERVATIONS, 1946

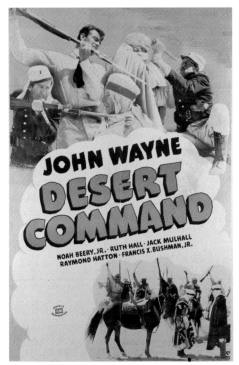

232. DESERT COMMAND, 1946

233. ANGEL AND THE BADMAN, 1947,
1959 reissue

231. WITHOUT RESERVATIONS, 1946,
1953 reissue

234. TYCOON, 1947

235. FORT APACHE, 1948

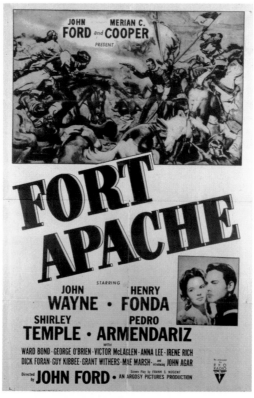

236. FORT APACHE, 1948, 1953 reissue

237. FORT APACHE, 1948, 1957 reissue

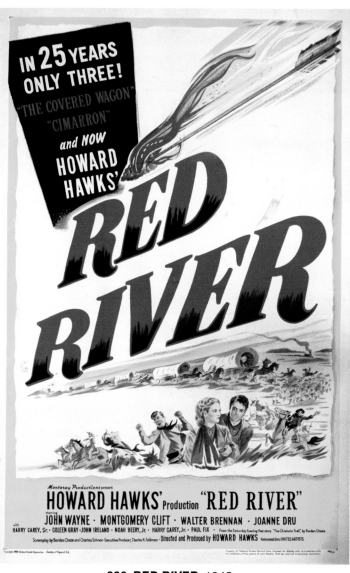

238. RED RIVER, 1948

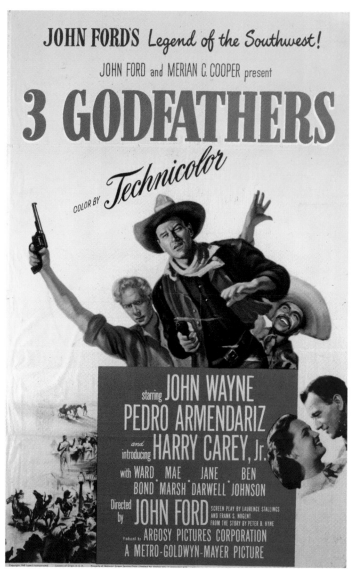

240. 3 GODFATHERS, 1949

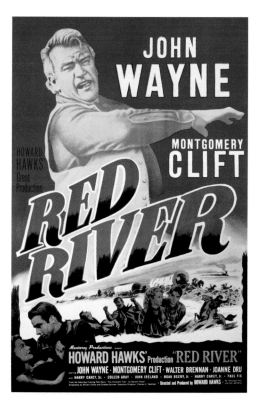

239. RED RIVER, 1948, 1952 reissue

241. 3 GODFATHERS, 1949, c.1962 reissue

242. WAKE OF THE RED WITCH, 1949

243. THE FIGHTING KENTUCKIAN, 1949

244. THE FIGHTING KENTUCKIAN,
1949, 1955 reissue

245. SHE WORE A YELLOW RIBBON,
1949, 1954 reissue

246. SHE WORE A YELLOW RIBBON,
1949, 1957 reissue

247. SHE WORE A YELLOW RIBBON, 1949

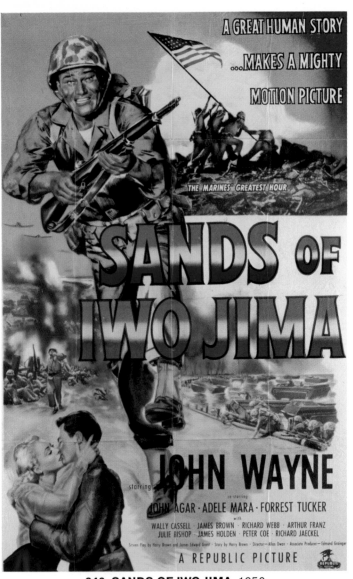

248. SANDS OF IWO JIMA, 1950

250. RIO GRANDE, 1950

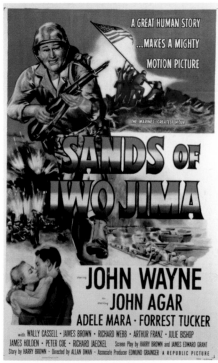

249. SANDS OF IWO JIMA, 1950,
1954 reissue

251. RIO GRANDE, 1950, 1956 reissue

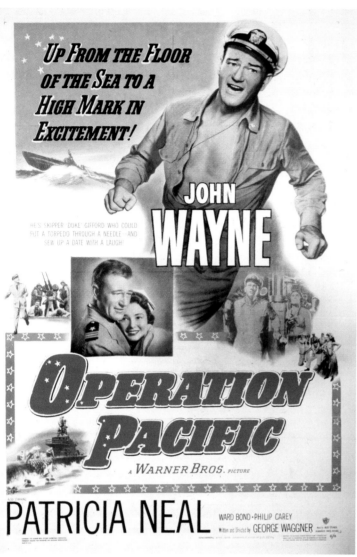

252. OPERATION PACIFIC, 1951

253. FLYING LEATHERNECKS, 1951

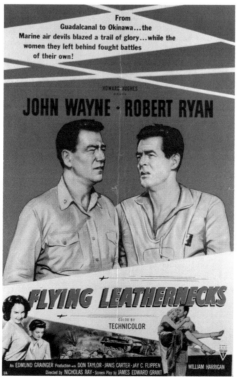

254. FLYING LEATHERNECKS, 1951,
1956 reissue

255. FLYING LEATHERNECKS, 1951,
1960s reissue

256. THE QUIET MAN, 1951

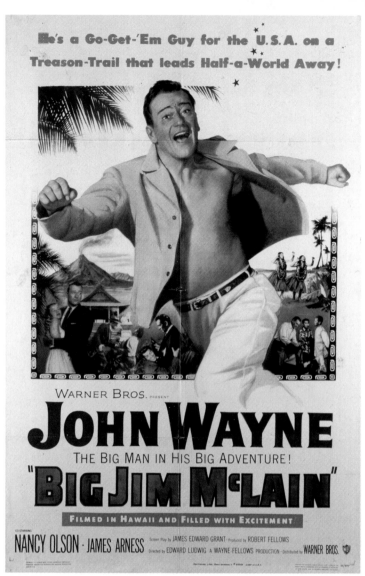

259. BIG JIM MCLAIN, 1952

257. THE QUIET MAN, 1951, 1956 reissue

258. THE QUIET MAN, 1951, 1957 reissue

260. HONDO, 1953

261. TROUBLE ALONG THE WAY, 1953

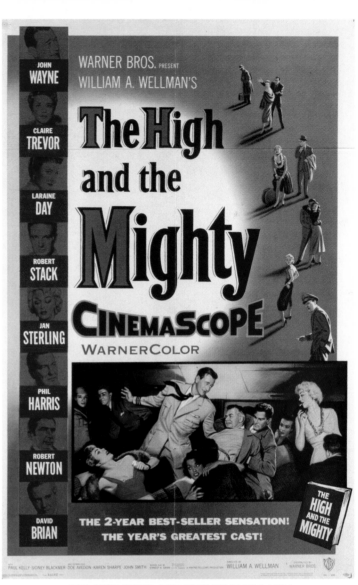

262. THE HIGH AND THE MIGHTY, 1954

263. ISLAND IN THE SKY, 1953

264. THE SEA CHASE, 1955

265. BLOOD ALLEY, 1955

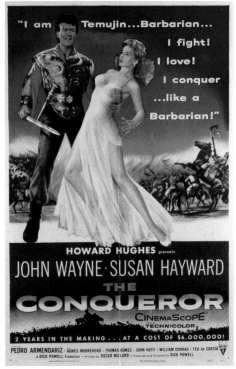

266. THE CONQUEROR, 1956

267. THE SEARCHERS, 1956, military one-sheet

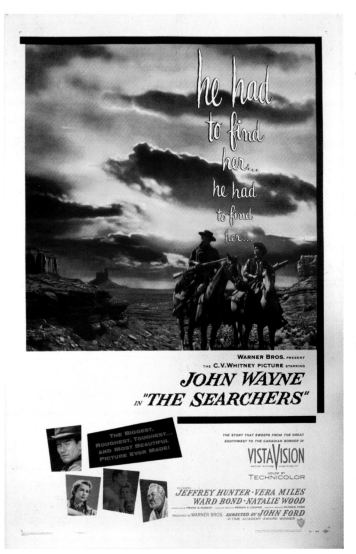

268. THE SEARCHERS, 1956

269-276. THE SEARCHERS, 1956 lobby cards

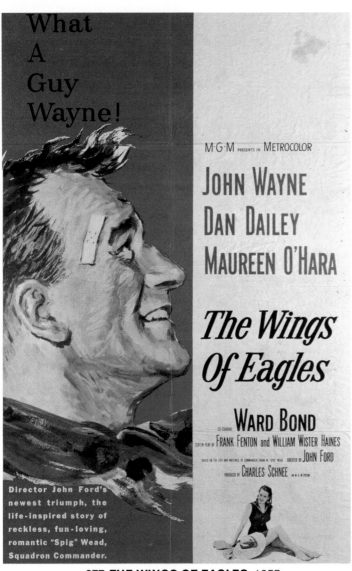

277. THE WINGS OF EAGLES, 1957

279. JET PILOT, 1957

278. THE WINGS OF EAGLES, 1957, 1966 reissue

280. JET PILOT, 1957, 1979 reissue

281. LEGEND OF THE LOST, 1957

282. THE BARBARIAN AND THE GEISHA, 1958

285. THE ALAMO, 1960

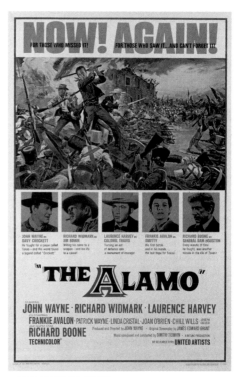

286. THE ALAMO, 1960, 1967 reissue

283. RIO BRAVO, 1959

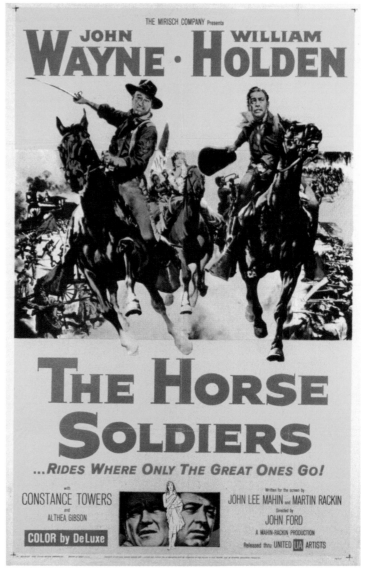

284. THE HORSE SOLDIERS, 1959

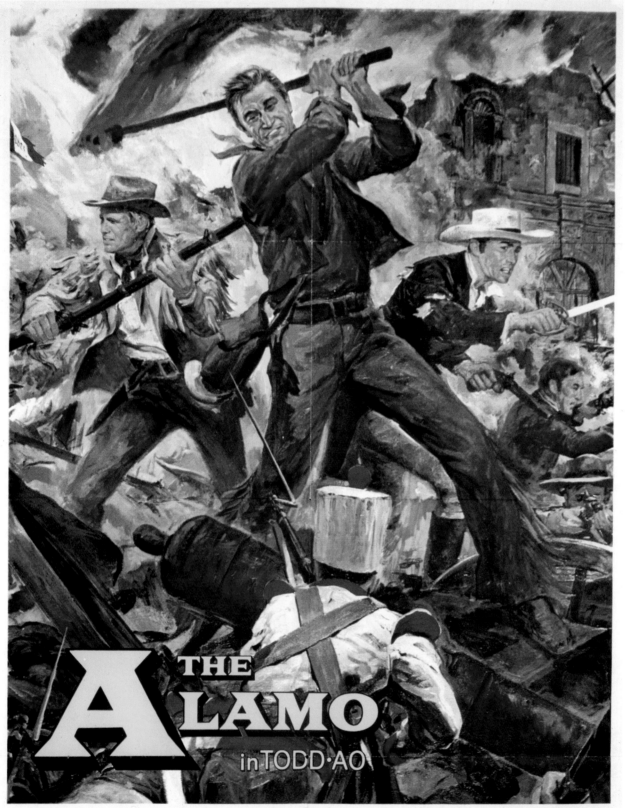

THE MISSION THAT BECAME A FORTRESS...THE FORTRESS THAT BECAME A SHRINE...

STARRING

JOHN WAYNE / RICHARD WIDMARK / LAURENCE HARVEY

CO-STARRING

FRANKIE AVALON   PATRICK WAYNE / LINDA CRISTAL   AND GUEST STAR
JOAN O'BRIEN / CHILL WILLS / JOSEPH CALLEIA   RICHARD BOONE

produced and directed by JOHN WAYNE / original screenplay by JAMES EDWARD GRANT
music composed and conducted by DIMITRI TIOMKIN / TECHNICOLOR
A BATJAC PRODUCTION RELEASED THROUGH UNITED ARTISTS

287. THE ALAMO, 1960, special TODD-AO one-sheet

288. NORTH TO ALASKA, 1960

290. THE COMANCHEROS, 1961

289. NORTH TO ALASKA, 1960, 1964 reissue

291. THE COMANCHEROS, 1961, 1960s reissue

292. THE MAN WHO SHOT LIBERTY VALANCE, 1962

293. HATARI, 1962

294. HATARI, 1962,
1960s reissue

295. HATARI, 1962,
1967 reissue

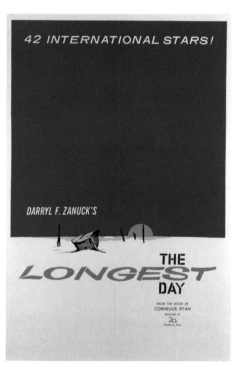

296. THE LONGEST DAY, 1962

297. THE LONGEST DAY, 1962

298. THE LONGEST DAY, 1962,
1969 reissue

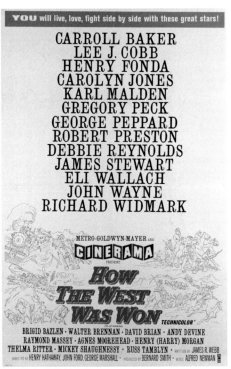

299. HOW THE WEST WAS WON, 1962

300. HOW THE WEST WAS WON, 1964

301. HOW THE WEST WAS WON, 1962,
1970 reissue

302. MCLINTOCK, 1963

303. DONOVAN'S REEF, 1963

304. CIRCUS WORLD, 1965

307. THE SONS OF KATIE ELDER, 1965

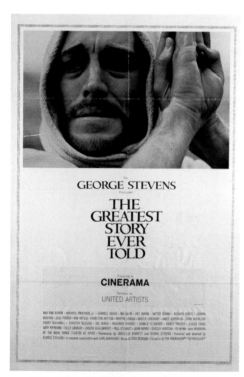

305. THE GREATEST STORY EVER TOLD, 1964

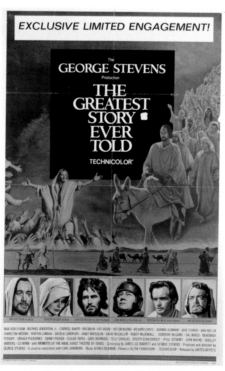

306. THE GREATEST STORY EVER TOLD, 1964

308. SONS OF KATIE ELDER/RED LINE 7000, double-bill release

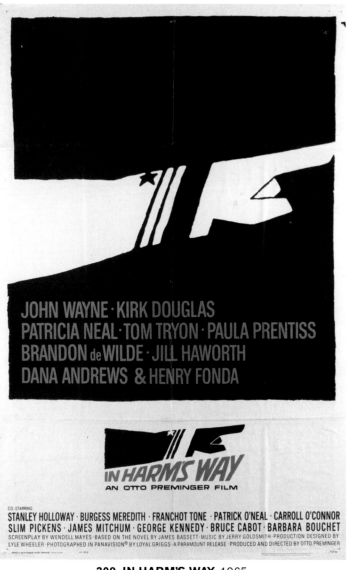

309. IN HARM'S WAY, 1965

310. CAST A GIANT SHADOW, 1966

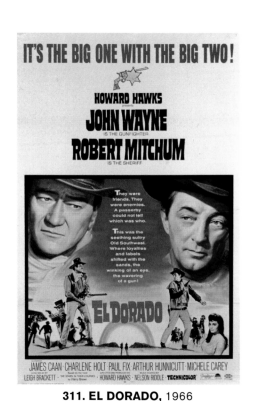

311. EL DORADO, 1966

312. THE WAR WAGON, 1967

313. THE GREEN BERETS, 1968

314. HELLFIGHTERS, 1969

315. TRUE GRIT, 1969,
"foreign" one-sheet

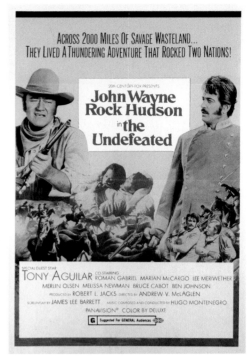

317. THE UNDEFEATED, 1969

316. TRUE GRIT, 1969

318. THE UNDEFEATED, 1969

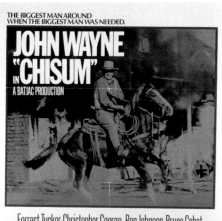

319. CHISUM, 1970   **320. CHISUM,** 1970   **322. BIG JAKE,** 1971

321. RIO LOBO, 1971   **323. BIG JAKE,** 1971

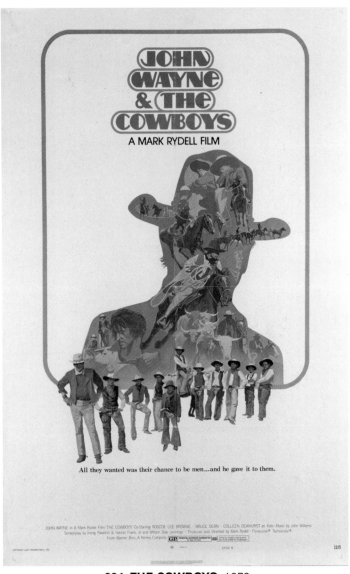

324. THE COWBOYS, 1972

326. CAHILL, 1973

325. THE COWBOYS, 1972

327. CAHILL, 1973

328. McQ, 1974

329. THE TRAIN ROBBERS, 1973

330. THE TRAIN ROBBERS, 1973

331. BRANNIGAN, 1975

332. BRANNIGAN, 1975

333. ROOSTER COGBURN, 1975

**He's got to face a gunfight once more
to live up to his legend once more
TO WIN JUST ONE MORE TIME.**

DINO DE LAURENTIIS presents
A FRANKOVICH/SELF Production

JOHN WAYNE
LAUREN BACALL

IN A SIEGEL FILM

"THE SHOOTIST"

Co-Starring RON HOWARD Guest Stars JAMES STEWART RICHARD BOONE JOHN CARRADINE SCATMAN CROTHERS
RICHARD LENZ HARRY MORGAN SHEREE NORTH HUGH O'BRIAN Music by ELMER BERNSTEIN
Screenplay by MILES HOOD SWARTHOUT and SCOTT HALE Based on the novel by GLENDON SWARTHOUT
Produced by M. J. FRANKOVICH and WILLIAM SELF Directed by DON SIEGEL Technicolor® A Paramount Release

76/165

334. THE SHOOTIST, 1976